Real Life
Poetry

Dr. William E. Smith

Real Life

Poetry

Dr. William E. Smith

WORKBOOK PRESS LLC
187 E Warm Springs Rd,
Suite B285 Las Vegas NV 89119 USA

Website: https://workbookpress.com/
Hotline: 1-888-818-4856
Email: admin@workbookpress.com

Ordering Information:

Quantity sales. Special discounts are available on quantity purchases by corporations, associations, and others. For details, contact the publisher at the address above.

Library of Congress Control Number:

ISBN-13:   978-1-965732-86-1   Paperback Version

REV. DATE: 06/12/2025

Dedication

"To Gladys, my amazing wife,
Dion, my son, and to Denise my goddaughter, whose
Unwavering support made this all possible.
This book is for you."

Contents

PROUD OF YOU

Look at you now – I'm so Proud of you-
Rejected by your friends and peers-
Turned out to be brighter than them all-
When they all laughed at you to shame-
Call you out of your name-
Nigger, black boy, poor trash – nothing.

I'm so proud of you.
Making the best out of nothing-
And becoming somebody-
No one ever dreamed of-
Yes! It's you – nigger, black boy, nothing-
Too Proud to be true.

Judged by the color of your skin.
Judged by your passing failures-
The drug addiction – the drunkard,
The beggar, the poor trash-
Look at you now.

You made it – through tough times.
Through the aces and pain-
The sunshine and rain-
Not what you use to be – you see-
I'm proud of you – nigger, Black boy, poor trash - nothing.

SHAKE YOURSELF OFF

Why sit around – and worry.
About pass failure-
Arise – shake yourself off.
And reach for the stars.

Life is too short – to worry.
Get up from this cold ground.
Wipe the tears from your eyes.
Dust yourself off – smile.
And climb to your feet – Repeat.

Face your destiny.
Determination; And will-
What's inside has always been-
Faith, Trust, Hope-
No one need to tell you-
It's there you see – still.

Shake yourself off – stand to your feet.
It's a new day – It's your time-
Leave your fears behind-
No one will ever know.
The real you inside
Shake Yourself Off – Shake Yourself Off.

TEARY EYE GIRL – BLUE EYE BABY

Honey – Peach Pie-
Is this your Teary eye girl-
Blue eye baby?
She doesn't look like you-
How can this be?
I just can't see.

What happened between you-
The midnight-
And the morning dew?
Are you insane?
Were you in the arms of some stranger
Who rocked your fantasy
And left you all alone?

Teary eye girl – Blue eye baby
Honey – Peach Pie
Where were you?
Between the sheets of pain-
Wrapped in the arms –
Of another man – users
How could this have been?
Now I understand – making love-
To another man – not your husband
It is a low-down rotten sin-
Got what you asked for – Teary eye girl – Blue eye baby.

HEY GIRL

Hey Girl-
Your life seemed to be-
Battled, bruised, and torn-
Between two lines of paper
Waiting for a new chapter-
To turn in your life.

You have had some dark days in your life-
Scattered by your pass-
It's time to come to your sense of reality-
Leaving your dark days behind.

It wasn't good for you to stay there-
It's time to move on to better things-
Nor turn back to broken pass-
Fragment of wasted years-
Hey Girl-

Cultivate that broken heart-
Let wisdom lead you farther on-
Your path to true success-
for God has intended for you-
to always to have the best.

DEATH A STEPPINGSTONE

Death is only one step-
From heaven's door-
The ground can no longer hold thee-
Thy soul is rushed to eternity-
Angels await – the gates of pearls-
To embrace thee to God's throne-
With their wings of love.

God everlasting kingdom – heaven-
There we all stand – women, and men-
Children of God – without sin-
Around His mighty throne-
Where the sun – forever shine no more-
Only God's Glory from above.

Death no longer reigns – over us-
In this old mortal body, no more-
From mortality to immortality-
Death is swallowed up in victory.

Let the lights of heaven shine-
The crown upon our heads a' rest-
Let eternal life begin a' fresh,
Forever upon our breast.

OUR LIFE

Our Life is counted for-
Like a needle on a clock-
Hanging on the wall, ticking down over time-
Night after night – recall-
Day after day – rewinds-
Cannot repeat what-
Has passed and gone on before.

No one knows – when-
It will come to its ending-
Only time will tell – It's new beginning-
As the years pass, We age.

Our Life ends – within time-
With tears of remembrance-
And hopes – of new beginning-
Taking off the old and putting on the new-
In a home we've all dreamed of-
Never, ever return – heaven.

PENNIES, NICKELS, DIMES

Have you ever-
Counted, Pennies, Nickels, and Dimes-
Like running through your veins – a million times-
If you could – would you, do it?
Over, and over-
Again, again.

The more I count, the richer I become-
The more I count – it's more, and some-

Until I run out of numbers, remember-
I will keep counting and just maybe-
I will have more – more – and just some-
Pennies, Nickels, Dimes.

TALKING CAT LENNY

Lenny talks with a Language-
You can understand-
He thinks he is human-
And very demand.

Early He rises in the morning-
At the same time – and calls your name-
He knows quite well!
It's breakfast time, can't you tell?

If He could fix His own food, he would've fixed-
Mash Potatoes – Chicken, and perhaps Gravy-
However, since he is a cat, he had to eat what was put on his table.

THE DEVIL ADVOCATE

Old man – what are you doing,
Sitting in this dark cold alley?
Smoking your pipe in tears-
When no one else see's you here-
Maybe lonesome 'uh, fears-
If not, then what?

You don't have to be lonesome, I'm here-
I'm here – to see you through-
What do you want me to do?
Come let's reason together, relax, yourself-
And embrace the time.

Tell me – no one, needs to know your story-
Only I can help you!
I took your dearest friend away from you – forever-
And I'll put you together again – just trust me.

Give me your soul – I'll will be with you always-
Through your darker hours, and bitter pain-
I'm the answer to your problem-
I will die for you – I will give you peace-
I will give you eternal life-
If you do what I have asked you to do-
Eternal life is only a fingertip away-
I will accompany you on that great judgment day.

Don't you worry anymore-
I will have the last and final say-
Had enough – self murder will ease your pain-

Take away your darkest hours-
We have been friends for years-
I'll make dying easy – and free you from your fears and tears.
You will escape this alley woe's – long nights of testing-
Bitter hours of depression – I am your advocate!
Who has fallen from heaven – I am numbered amongst the stars-
I am the world's best Prince – now I have gain them all-
Come, bow down before me – I have much to give thee.

Soon you will be done with the troubles of this world-
In one second – your life will flash before you – and you will be free.

Look here! The gun you have in your hand, put it to your head-
Pull the trigger on the gun-
Bang, Bang, Bang, you're dead – you are now done-
My friend, I am who I am – My name is death and hell-
Sorry, you couldn't tell – Lucifer.

No Place Like Home

You left home – to a place of no face,
A fugitive with no space – and no one knew you there-
Sleeping on the cold night ground – no pillow resting upon your head-
Only a face full of frowns – no friends to greet-
Only lonesome strangers you meet.

Everyone seems to pass you by – Only the dark night sky-
Your past never ever stopped haunting you-
It was a decision you made.

A shelter from the stormy blast – the twinkling of the stars-
The moon, the sun, smiles upon you, disappears in its laughter-
As they exchange their temperament – the day from the night.

Early in the morning you could hear the alarm clock.
It's breakfast, it's the smell of dew, coffee, eggs, and waffles too-
The dawn of a new day arise – No place like home-
I think I will arise, I'll go back to my father's house-
There's an old rotten couch, a table with three legs-
A chair with no pegs – A bed with no mattress, plates with no forks-
And a refrigerator full of food.

I'll walk, I'll talk, better than never – ever – I see!
It's a house with squeaking floors – broken glass windows, and a leaky roof.
The food is not at my expense – better than worse it's best – Nothing but a test!
What do I have to lose, the choice is mine – and today is the right time-
To change my mind. There is no place like home - I will arise-
It's more than worth waiting for – sleeping with the mouse on the couch-
I'll tolerate the best I can, Responsibility is only for a man-
If I can take it, I surely will make it-
No Place Like Home.

Same Old Stuff

I'm tired of the same old stuff-
It's time for a change, dealing with problems that never rest-
Retiring is wonderful – only if you can find yourself-
Engaged with true happiness.

I know not what each day will bring-
I just keep moving toward my destiny – tracing after my identity-
Trying to find my uncertainty.

In the twinkling of an eye – years just keeps on passing by-
Same old Stuff – It's rough – tough-
Same Old Stuff – Same Old Stuff.

I'VE NEVER WENT TO HEAVEN

I've Never Went to Heaven, but I know it's so true-
Jesus said, He's coming back – just for me and for you-
I've Never Went to Heaven, but I know it's so real-
When I stand before my God, everything will be revealed.
No one has gone to heaven to tell me; how Beautiful it may be-
When I look around each day, I can surely, surely, see.

The moon, the stars that shine, and the beauty of the sky.
God presence is everywhere; His presence will never die.

I've Never Went to Heaven – but I have been told-
The streets up there is paved with pure gold-
And one day will surely come, we all be going home.

I've Never Went to Heaven, but I believe there's such a place-
When I stand before my God, I will see Him face to face.

And I'll be there in heaven, in that beautiful place-
Oh' Yes, my dear friend, He is the beginning and the end.
I Have Never Went to Heaven; It's waiting around the bend.

A GREAT FALLING AWAY

Theres a great falling away – in all the churches today-
People come, and People go – they may not come back anymore-
And I wonder what's on their mind-
It seems although they're marking time, I wonder-
If Jesus would come today, would they be left behind?

There's a great falling away – in all of our churches today-
The same faithful few, sitting there on the pew-
Is time running out on you?
Maybe you don't know what to do, come back to the church-
My sisters, and brothers, the Lord is in need of you-
He has not forgotten you.

I wonder what's on your mind, I hope you are doing find-
Oh' come back to church – My sisters, and brothers,
Don't you be left behind?

No Time to Give Up

You've been praising God for a long time-
Why are you leaving now?
The ground that you are standing on is Holy ground-
You can't let anyone run you away, no matter what they say-
Stand still, firm in His word, let your voice be heard-
God will reward you in that great judgment day.

The Lord has been good to you, no matter what you do-
Jesus will soon give a shout; it's no time to bail out-
God will surely see you through. Trouble will come, and trouble will go-
Jesus will soon be knocking at your heart door-
So! Stand still firm, and keep walking by faith-
And the day will come when you enter that pearly gate-
No Time to Give Up.

I STILL BELIEVE IN YOU

Today seems as though when we first begun-
When I use to hold you in my arms, and yesterday has come and gone-
But I Still Believe in You.

Although we are turning old and gray, it still seems as though it was yesterday-
When we first began. Our love has not faded away – I Still Believe in You.

You're the one I'm still holding on too, because I Still Believe in You-
Although sometimes we disagree, I and you, and you and me-
Only because I Still Believe in You, and you believe in me.

BORN TO BE A PREACHER

I never thought I would turn out to be the person I am you see-
My mom prayers reached my heart gently, as she rocked me upon her knees-
I was too young to even know which way my life would go-
When I was born, that Preacher man said, if you name that boy after me-
He will grow up and be that Preacher boy you see.

Now this old Preacher man is dead and gone-
And my mom has left me alone; she is now gone-
I wonder if he had never died, would this ever become true, beside-
I didn't want to be – you see, God had his hands on me-
Like that old Preacher man, God had him in the palm of his hands.
My life was not planned by the old Preacher man you see-
The Spirit of God had its hands on me-
The old Preacher man only spoke it into reality-
Born to be the Preacher I am supposed to be.

OLD AGE

Old age is like sitting in a wheelchair thinking about how to start it up-
And I can never find the keys-
However, stay stationary until you unlock the wheels, being unaware.

SO! My unfamiliar friends – old age – you just can't win-
Don't forget to put your teeth in before you eat and roll back the cover
before you fall to sleep-
Don't forget to put the stocking cap on your head before getting into bed.

If your thoughts are lost and they are hard to find, don't give-
Up on the lost memories of your mind – just get into the bed-
The best way you can, forget about your head at the foot of the bed-
It just isn't screwed on tight – turn out the lights, kiss yourself good night-
And say, good night, good night, something just isn't right.

I HAVE COME A LONG WAY

I Have Come a Long Way-
When black was my negro's name -
And nigger was blacker than blue-
Was it a white man's game – giving me this name?

From the dark days of slavery-
Through the cotton fields of Georgia-
From my African Ancestry – I Have Come a Long Way-
From West and Central Africa – to the Americas during -
The Transatlantic Slave Trades. From the American South-
To Northern, Midwestern, and Western States-
During the great Migration, and depression-
I Have Come a Long Way – cannot go back, I must stay.

All my friends are black and white; we are all precious in God sight-
I've migrated from the South – when life was bitter than lemon – sugar honey-
I came to the North – free – no money. From the white man's pain – through-
The storm and the rain, beaten by whips, locked up in chain-
I Have Come a Long Way.

You knew me there – you brought here – and I just don't care-
Remember you brought me here by boat, cargo, and train-

Nigger, is that my real birth name? I wonder what my real name is.
Is it Nigger, Negro, Black, or color people?
Is it black, blue, is it brown, or is those slave-
Owner's names still floating around downtown?
Is It a White man's name, or a white man's game?
I Have Come a Long Way.

DARK AS THE NIGHT

Dark as the night-
Bright as the stars glitter-
And bright as the moon shines-
Beaming upon the face of another-
The sun sets upon the day morning dew,
As the break of dawn appears, brings forth the day.

Patches of green grass, brown leaves as puzzles-
Upon the cold ground many shapes are fashionable, colors, and foams.
Can you hear the drop of water as they fall from the sky?

Wetting the umbrella, covered heads,
As we walk along this muddy road.
The birds are singing in the trees, voices of many melodies.

Dancing across the ocean breeze-
I sit down to rest upon this old, hollowed stump-
After miles of walking – may I taste the fresh air-
As it blows upon my chest, breathe.

I'm looking back from whence I came, a long way back-
From where I started from.
My destiny is only one day more, miles, miles, and miles-

My feet are tired and sore – Dark as the night.
I must continue this journey-
Dark as the night in this cold cloudy weather.
It seems so far away-
No one was walking beside me.

Mountains and hills I must climb to reach my destiny-
Then I will lie down-
And rest my head upon my pillow,
And take my last breath-
Never have to travel this way again.

WHEN JESUS STEPS OUT ON THE CLOUD

The day will surely come when Jesus will call us home-
Gabriel will blow that trumpet so loud-
Jesus will step out on the Cloud-
Every eye will see him; every knee shall bow-
And everyone will see His shining face.

His feet will not touch the ground; there is so much sin around-
Every building standing – He will bring them all down-
When Jesus steps out on the Cloud.
Old things will pass away, and it will be a brand-new day-
When all our sins will be washed away.

Whether day or night; there will be a great glorying light-
Shining from the heavens, heavens, above-
The trumpet will sound loud – He'll step out on the cloud-
Jesus will Step out on the Cloud.

The day will surely come – you'll gain the victory-
When Jesus Steps out on the Cloud – Every eye will see Him-
And every knee shall bow – Jesus will step out on the Cloud.
His feet will not touch the ground – there is too much sin around-
When Jesus Steps out on the Cloud.

GOD IS FAITHFUL

God is Faithful, He's faithful to you-
God is Faithful, He's faithful to you-
No matter what you're going through.
God is Faithful to you; God is Faithful to you.

No matter what you say or do; every word of God is true-
He's faithful; He's faithful to you-
Sometimes you're so wrong – and sometimes you're head strong.
But – God has been so faithful to you.

Don't you ever let Him down; He'll aways be around-
He will be with you through thick and thin; He'll be with you until the end-
God has been faithful, faithful to you.

Sometimes you were sick and tired, but God was standing right by your side.
He's faithful, faithful to you.
No matter what you say or do, I am a witness – I am a witness too-
God has been faithful to you.

THE SONG OF MY DREAMS

You're the song of my dreams-
You're always on my mind-
I can see you no matter where I am-
You're the song of my dreams.

When I open my eyes – you catch me by surprise-
As I gaze toward the sky – you're the hope of my fears-
You're the drops of my tears – I can sense you in my heart-
You're always on my mind.

I can see you no matter where I am,
Because you meant so much to me-
You bring back old memories, although you are gone-
You will always be my song – You're the song of my dreams-
No matter where I am because you meant so much to me.
The Song of my Dreams.

REMEMBERING MAMA

He stands by the old table, on the corner of exhaustion-
Sipping slowly with – a hot cup of coffee in his hand.
Enjoying the times he once remembered.

Looking through his broken lens – frame of his glasses-
And his eyes gazing toward the sunlight shining.
Upon the worn countertop.

His mother left a legacy behind, so he tried to dance in her shoes.
While keeping the pace – the melody of her songs alive-
Upon his face – he smiles.

Wrinkled, and torn – his – bleached, and faded blue jeans-
Hanging below his belly button, his hands trembling at the cup-
Sits down to drink, singing to himself over, and over again-
Then he smiles – Remembering Mama.

HOMELESS MAN

He slept in his car – on the back seat, trying to keep warm-
With tears in his eyes hoping to see the dawn of a new day.
He stood there on the street – when the days were long cold.
The temperature hot – begging for food, with his old cap in his hand-
While everyone seems to pass him by.

He kept standing there, by the old light poll on the side of the road-
Waiting his final turn homeless, no clothes to wear – no food to eat-
No shoes to put on his feet – no place to lay his head.

A stranger no one knew, then finally his break came-
Someone stops to supply his needs, he smiles and says thank you.

The next time I come back everyone will know who I am-
Keep your eyes on the cloud, the trumpet will sound loud-
Only homeless for now – Homeless Man – Jesus!!!

I'll Still be Me

Laugh at me – make me cry-
Wet my eyes with your tears – I'll Still be Me-
Smack my face with your dirty nasty words – I'll Still be Me.

I'm strong as the paw of a loin – the strength of a killer whales jaw-
I'm tall as an old oak tree – when the wind blows-
Knock me down to my knees – I'll Still be Me.

Make fun of me – I'll still be me – throw me your curve ball of lies-
You may hit me between my eyes – I'll Still be Me - You'll see.

My Mama didn't raise no jelly back chicken – nor did she raise a wimp.
I won't go down without a fight, if I come back with a limp – I'll Still be Me.

Laugh at me - make me cry – push me to the ground – I'll still be standing-
I'll Still be Me – you see.

OVER DRAWN ACCOUNT

Went to the bank – to draw some money-
The bank teller asked, "Are you trying to be funny?
There is no money here in your account-
Every check you wrote, bounced, bounced, bounced.

All your accounts are passed due – and the check you just wrote bounced too-
I just don't know what you're going to do – if you don't pay – we're going to sue.

There is no money left to cover your bills; late charges are due-
And fees are pending against you – there is nothing else we can do – but-

Close out the account, and leave us alone – all that money you had-
Is gone, gone, gone – faster it came – faster it went – all you did was
spent, spent, spent.

WHITE BREAD BLACK BREAD

I told you; you have it made in the shade-
You're eating your white bread now-
Better enjoy it while you can, sooner you will be leaving on your own-
And the bread you're now eating will be gone.

The minute you step out of that front door-
You'll bump your head – you'll stump your toe-
Working your fingers to the bone-
The bill collectors won't leave you alone.

If you don't have money to buy the bread-
Just keep on remembering, white bread – black bread-

Whatever comes – whatsoever may-
If you want to keep eating that white bread-
You'll have to pay.
White Bread, Black Bread, nothing from nothing, leaves nothing.

LEFTOVERS

Little boy says to his father – Pop's I'm tired of eating Leftovers.
Father said – That is just what it is – Leftovers, Leftovers-
Is better than nothing at all – little boy says to his father-
Is that all we got?

Father says to the little boy – Thank God – We do have-
A Table, a Chair, a Pot, and I have gotten to the place I just don't care.
My teeth are falling out – And even my hair – turning gray.

If I were as hungry as you – I would eat that chicken, and potato stew.
Leftovers – Leftovers – something is better than nothing-
And while you're eating – you ought to thank God for something.

SOME FOLKS

Some Folks goes to church just to sit and look around-
While others go to church to put other people down.
Some Folks goes to church just to jump and shout-
While others go to church to lay other people out.

Some Folks goes to church to hear what the Preacher say-
While others go to church to turn others away.

If you go to church – And your heart just isn't right-
You're still walking in darkness – you need to come to the light-
Give your life to Jesus – while you're in your right mind-
Give your life to Jesus, while you have time-
Some Folks – Church Folks.

FRIEND TO FRIEND

Hey man, you haven't worked a day in your life-
What are you going to do? With all those children and no wife?
If I keep spending my tax dollars on you-
I would be begging, borrowing; and I will be left broke too.

I am not a bank – nor financial institution – and I am not the answer-
Nor your solution. As of today, don't ask me for no more money.
I'm not your Daddy – I'm not your Honey.

Stop calling me on the telephone if you can't make it on your own.
Sorry my friend, just leave me alone. Hey man you're so wrong, wrong, wrong.
Just leave me alone, please just leave me alone. I'm hanging up the phone!!!

LANDLORD TO RENTER

Landlord to Renter – look! I'm trying to help you-
But you always hit – and – miss – hit – and – miss-
You started out paying – find – your rent was paid on time-
What happened? Did you forget to pay?

From Jan – thru – the month of May – your rent is overdue-
And I am getting rid of you.

Renter to Landlord – look hear, I am sorry Sir, I am doing the best I can-
With the little money I have – only working part time at the coffee stand-
Eating food out of the garbage can – I don't have no money in my hand.

Landlord to Renter – the winter has come and gone – spring has also passed-
And the summer, is now on – you have a month – to – month – lease-
And by the first of next month, I expect you to be gone.

Renter to Landlord – Mister – Mister – please don't put me out on the street-
I will have no place to go – and I have no money-
To buy anything to eat.

Landlord to Renter – Well! Maybe we can work something out-
Work something out – just pay me my money – ah' just get going – shut up-
And move out – That's what it's all about – I've just worked it out –
just worked it out-
That's what it's all about – just worked it out.
Living in my house just isn't free – all that money you owed me –
move out – move out-
That's what it's all about.

DEBTOR

I'm not the boss – I just pay the cost – I am human just like you-
Trying to catch up on my bills – hoping I will soon have a breakthrough-
I'm short on money – And the bills are coming in fast – one bill is due today-
And another one is due tomorrow – my credit cards are up to its limit-
I don't know how long this will last.

No banks for me to borrow from – interest rates are killing me softly-
And there is no excuse for me – I am as busted as can be-
I can't see myself getting ahead – as fast as the money comes in-
It goes out of my hands again.

Many years has come and gone, and the bills are still lingering on-
The debt I owe is extremely high – It seem as though it reaches the sky-
I guess my co-worker will pay it – when I close my eyes and die.
When I close my eyes and die – when I close my eyes and die!

UNEMPLOYED

I lost my job – no later than yesterday – the unemployment office was closed-
Told me – come back another day – I got so mad – with myself-
Until I didn't know what to do.
My wife was sick in bed – And my children all had the flu.

I went to borrow some money – from a friend I once knew – he didn't
have any money-
He was out of his job too.

THAT'S LIFE

When you make plans – and things doesn't turn out right – that's life-
When you put money away – for a rainy day – and your air conditioner-
breaks down in the month of May – and you have no money –
but you must pay-
That's life.

When you go to the grocery store – to buy some food – and you spent
more money-
Then you wanted to – that's life – when the bills come tumbling in
your mailbox-
And your money seems to be on the rocks – That's Life.

When you're driving – on a lonesome road – your car breaks down –
on the other side-
Of town – and you look up – there is no one around-
And every service station has closed – that's life – just remember-
You are not the only person that's going through – maybe –
God have a better plan-
For you – That's Life.

I just don't Understand

Why do you curse me out – around and about – blaspheme my name-
In the middle of the street in front of my friends – and those we meet-
I just don't understand.

I've given you that shirt – off my back, you even used my Cadillac.
I've given you money.
I've given you shoes – the things you say about me, just isn't good news.
I just don't Understand.

When you said, you love me – you talk about me behind my back-
Say things about me – I just don't like – lies to me in front of my face-
Calls me names – out of my race, I just don't Understand.

I need to find some other place to go – give me the car keys, and let me go-
We just can't get along anymore – I just don't Understand.

You Don't Know Everything

If you think that you know everything-
Can you count the stars – if you think you know everything-
Can you tell me – who lives on Mars?

If you think you know everything – can you count the raindrops-
That falls from the sky – and the very day – the hour -when you will die.
You Don't Know Everything.

If you think that you know everything – can you tell me-
How far is heaven away? The month – the year of judgment day-
You Don't Know Everything.

If you think you know everything – can you tell me – how many
people are now dead-
when the sun turns from yellow to red – or count the number of hairs
on your head-
You Don't Know Everything.

You may be dressed down from your head to your knees-
You may have all those college degrees, but you don't know everything-
You can't tell me what your ending will be – you just don't know
everything.
The problem with you, you know too much – but you don't know
everything-
Nor do you know what the next day will bring.
Start looking around yourself – Stop pointing fingers at me-
If you keep on living – you will see – You Don't Know Everything.

A CAT IN THE HOUSE

When there is a cat in the house-
You don't have to worry – about the mouse.
He will flip him over – knock him down – and stretch him out-
That's what's it all about.

When there is a cat in the house – I feel sorry for the mouse-
He may duck and hide – but the cat knows how to thrive-
He will flip him over – knock him down – and stretch him out-
That's what's it all about.

FIGHTING, FUSSING, AND CUSSING

Fighting, Fussing, and Cussing – not getting any better-
Fighting, Fussing, and Cussing – you're surely breaking my heart.
Fighting, Fussing, and Cussing –   seems like you just don't care-
Fighting, Fussing, and Cussing – you're surely not getting anywhere.

It seems as though life has done me wrong – didn't know you was Gone-
Turn out to be this way. When we joined hands together – on that sun
shiny day.
In May – Fighting, Fussing, and Cussing – is not what I wanted this to be-
Will you please take your hands off me, I am going back to Germany-
That's where I need to be. Germany, Germany!

A TROUBLED WORLD

Look at this world my people; what was on your mind?
Going to the polls to vote, for an Authoritarian, Autocratic,
a hater, a dictator. Only to suffer the consequence of this later – a decline.

A man who was convicted on 34 felonies who is one of our worst enemies-
A President, who cares only about himself – not concern about anyone else-
Look at this world, my people, you have made a very terrible choice-
And now he doesn't even hear your voice.

A leader who exercises authority – in a coercive, tyrannical way-
And doesn't care what anyone says. He is imperious, commands, and
demands-
Wants to rewrite the Constitution – and don't have any common solution-
What is our resolution?

Our world is in deep trouble – the cost of living has double-
America U.S. dollar has diminished-
And his term in the Oval Office has not finished.

We are all standing on the world stage – it's time to turn the page-
We are facing some unprecedented – dark and dreary days.
The night is far spent – the day is at hand, wars, and chaos across this land-
God repented, that He even created man.

Putin is a disgrace to humanity – Trump has lost his insanity-
And Ukraine needs emergency – fighting to protect democracy.

Conflict and instability – on the uprise – wars in Africa,
Europe, and the Middle East, has caught all of us by surprise.
What this world needs now is peace.

Russia, China, and North Korea – are next door neighbors-
Supporting this war with bad behavior; causing this world to become
unstable.
We need to be released from this war – with compromise, and good favor.

This economy has gotten worse – than we expected-
With rising inflation still, a concern – this world is in a series of
concession-
Fears of a downturn of economic recession – leading us all to a total
depression-
Let us turn our plates down – fast and pray – keep trusting in God-
He will make away – in this trouble world.

SIGNS OF THE TIME

We are living in times of accelerating change of uncertainty-
A rapid advancement in technology, digital landscape of cyber
insecurity-
This world faces profound instability from climate change,
to geopolitical conflicts – in times which the Bible predicts-
Increase in wars – famines – earthquakes-
A world full of intense headaches.

Pestilences, diseases are on the uprise – high gas prices-
food, all a surprise, selfishness, ungratefulness, and lawlessness-
religious deception, persecution, and unforgiveness.
Signs are in the heavens – a time of perception – and rejection.

We are living in times of a divided nation, and inflation-
Immigration, stagnation, intimidation- in fabrication, and false
information-
We can all see the signs of the time, and serious crimes-
Will you be ready when Christ appear? The promise He made is very near-
No time to worry – no time to fear – it's real – it's clear-
It's the sound in this world ear – "Signs of the Time".

www.ingramcontent.com/pod-product-compliance
Lightning Source LLC
Chambersburg PA
CBHW051246120626
46547CB00014B/1820